P9-DCP-377

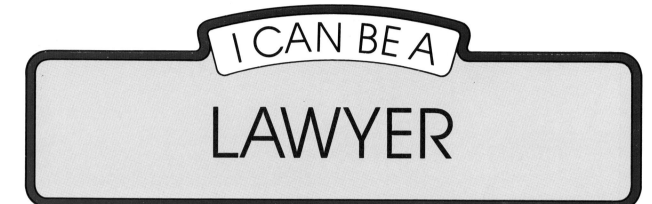

I CAN BE A

LAWYER

By Marlene Targ Brill

Prepared under the direction of Robert Hillerich, Ph.D.

CHILDRENS PRESS ®

CHICAGO

Library of Congress Cataloging in Publication Data

Brill, Marlene Targ.
   I can be a lawyer.

   Includes index.
   Summary: Easy-to-read text examines the duties of
various types of lawyers and the educational
requirements of a career in law.
   1. Law—Vocational guidance—United States—Juvenile
literature. [1. Law—Vocational guidance.   2. Vocational
guidance.   3. Occupations]
I. Title.
KF297.Z9B68   1987   340'.023'73   87-13227
ISBN 0-516-01911-2

To Alison, who can be whatever she wants

Childrens Press®, Chicago
Copyright ©1987 by Regensteiner Publishing Enterprises, Inc.
All rights reserved. Published simultaneously in Canada.
Printed in the United States of America.
1 2 3 4 5 6 7 8 9 10 R 96 95 94 93 92 91 90 89 88

PICTURE DICTIONARY

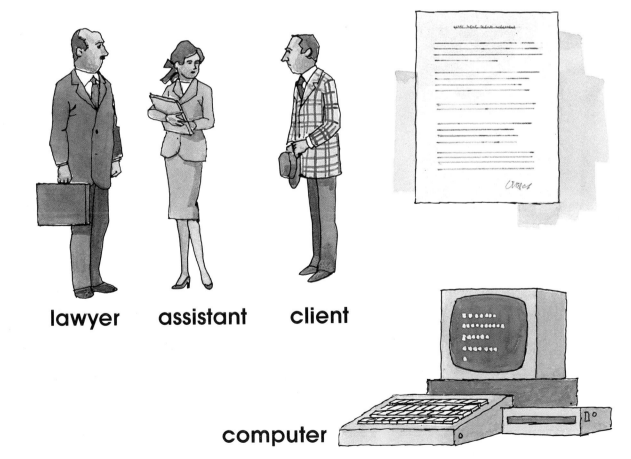

contract

lawyer   assistant   client

computer

judge

jury

court

BRENNER,
JOHNSON,
FIDDLE, DYRA
& SMITH

law firm

law library

Traffic signs (above) are used to tell people what they can and cannot do.
When a driver breaks a traffic law he or she will get a ticket.

Did you know that there are rules, called laws, to keep you safe? There are laws that say how schools should be run. There are laws that say how skyscrapers can be built. Laws are written to protect people.

Lawyers help you know which laws are for you

lawyer

Lawyers help people who are in trouble.

and your family. They let
you know what you can
and cannot do under the
law.

When two people do
not agree about what is
right, lawyers help them
put together a fair
agreement. Lawyers write

Lawyers help two people agree on a written contract.

everything about this agreement in a contract. The contract becomes a law for these two people to follow.

contract

Sometimes two people cannot agree about who is right under the law. They go to court.

judge

jury

court

client

In court a judge or jury of many people is asked to decide. One lawyer talks for each side. The judge or jury hears all the facts from the lawyers. Then they make a decision. The people must follow what the court decides.

People who hire lawyers are called clients. Clients

A jury (above left) is sworn in. Lawyers (top right and below) present their cases before a judge in a courtroom.

Lawyers work for people who are called clients.

may be one person or a group of persons.

One lawyer may have a client who wants to open her own store. Another lawyer's client may be a family who wants to sell a business.

Many families use lawyers to help them buy a house.

Big companies can be clients, too. Companies hire lawyers to write their contracts with other companies or people. Lawyers help companies do business in other countries, too. Lawyers help companies run their business.

Towns or cities can have lawyers. Lawyers

This lawyer is appealing the decision of a lower court. He is asking the panel of judges to reconsider his client's case.

help them write laws for their community. Lawyers read the contracts and agreements the town or city might make with other people. Lawyers talk for the town or city in court.

In all cases, lawyers

Lawyers work very hard.

want their clients to be
treated fairly. They want
them to be treated the
same under the law.

Think about the lawyers
you see on television. How
do they work? What do
they need to know?

Clients must give their lawyers all the facts.

First, lawyers meet with clients in homes, offices, or jails. They talk about the law and their clients' rights. Together the lawyers and their clients decide what to do.

All lawyers use law books. In Great Britain lawyers
who present cases in higher courts are called barristers.
They wear wigs and black robes.

Then lawyers look up laws in law libraries. They find other cases that are similar to their client's case.

law library

computer

Some lawyers use computers to find this information. They put these facts together in a way that best helps their client. Computers help lawyers write contracts and other papers from these facts.

Today many lawyers use computers to help them prepare their cases for court.

Sometimes lawyers meet with the judge privately (above) in what is called the judge's chambers. At other times they talk to him quietly in court.

Sometimes, lawyers talk to the lawyers on the other side. They may not want their client to go to court. So they try to settle the case before this happens. However, when a case goes to court, each lawyer speaks for his or her client. Each lawyer wants to win the case for his or her client.

Sometimes lawyers must work at night.

Lawyers like working
with people. They know
where to find facts and
how to put them together
at a later time. Lawyers
must be good readers
and writers.

The court reporter takes down every word
that is said in the courtroom.

Lawyers must be quick
thinkers. They must ask the
right questions. Lawyers
often have to change
people's ideas in order to
win the case for their
clients.

Future lawyers finish high school and at least three years of college. After college, they take a test to get into law school. In law school they study laws and court decisions. They learn how to present a case in court. They study law for three years. After law school they must take another test to be a lawyer.

Opposite page: A law professor explains a point of law to students.

23

Young lawyers learn from more experienced lawyers.

law firm

BRENNER,
JOHNSON,
FIDDLE, DYRA
& SMITH

assistant

Beginning lawyers usually work for other lawyers in law firms as assistants. They look for facts and write some contracts.

Some lawyers work in criminal court.

After lawyers learn about many different laws, they may specialize. Some lawyers work at one kind of law only, such as tax law or criminal law.

Most judges were lawyers. They know the law
and how lawyers should present cases in court.

Sometimes two lawyers will represent a single client in court.

Lawyers who specialize work for themselves, large law firms, businesses, or government.

Many lawyers do not specialize. They need to know all types of law. They are in general law.

27

Judges must listen very carefully. If they want to "refresh" their memory about what was said in court they can read the record kept by the court reporter (right).

The Bill of Rights is part of the Constitution of the United States. It says that everyone accused of a crime has the right to a fair trial. No matter where they work, lawyers help clients get a fair trial.

A young boy answers the lawyer's questions.

Lawyers help people protect their rights. They want you and your family to know that laws can work for you.

WORDS YOU SHOULD KNOW

accuse (ah • KYOOZ)—to blame; to charge someone with a crime or other wrongdoing

agreement (ah • GREE • ment)—arrangement, as a contract, between two or more sides

assistants (ah • SISS • tents)—helpers

business (BIZ • ness)—a store, trade, factory, anything set up to sell products or services

clients (KLY • ents)—persons for whom a lawyer provides his services; customers

community (kuh • MYOO • nih • tee)—people living under the same government or in the same area

contract (KAHN • trakt)—often prepared by a lawyer, a written agreement between two or more persons which when signed by all parties becomes enforceable by law

court (KORT)—a room where arguments are heard before a judge and often a jury

crime (KRYME)—a person's illegal action punishable by laws of the community or higher government

criminal law (KRIM • ih • nil LAW)—law dealing with crime and the punishment due

INDEX

PHOTO CREDITS

© Cameramann International Ltd.—Cover, 4 (top center & bottom), 9 (bottom), 13 (left), 14, 15 (right), 17 (2 photos)

EKM-Nepenthe—26 (bottom)
© John Maher—9 (top right), 10, 26 (top), 28 (left)

Gartman Agency:
© Ellis Herwig—6, 25

Journalism Services:
© Joseph Jacobson—4 (top right)

Mary Messenger—28 (right)

Nawrocki Stock Photo:
© Jim Wright—4 (top left)
© Robert Lightfoot III—24
© Jeff Apoian—27

Odyssey Productions:
© Robert Frerck—22

H. Armstrong Roberts:
©Camerique—7, 9 (top left), 13 (right), 18 (2 photos), 21, 29
©A. Teufen—15 (left)
©Gardon/Reflection—20 (left)
©Seghers 2—20 (right)

AP/Wide World Photos—12

ABOUT THE AUTHOR

Marlene Targ Brill is a free-lance Chicago-area writer, specializing in fiction and nonfiction books, articles, media, and other educational materials for children. Among her credits are biographical contributions to *World Book Encyclopedia's The President's World* and social studies and science articles for *Encyclopedia Britannica.* Ms. Brill holds a B.A. in Special Education from the University of Illinois and an M.A. in Early Childhood Education from Roosevelt University. She currently writes for health care, business, and young people's publications, and is active in Chicago Women in Publishing and Independent Writers of Chicago. *Encyclopedia of Presidents: John Adams* was her first book for *Childrens Press.*

decision (dih • SIJ • un)—a conclusion reached after considering facts and explanations

facts (FAKTS)—truth, something that can be proved

future (FYOO • cher)—to come; not yet arrived

hire (HY • er)—employ

judge (JUHJ)—public official authorized to hear and decide cases presented in his or her court

jury (JOO • ree)—a group of persons selected and sworn to hear a case and give a verdict based on the evidence presented in court

lawyer (LOY • er)—a person qualified to offer legal advice to clients and to represent them in court

present (preh • ZENT)—to offer to a court for a hearing and a decision

settle (SET • il)—to end a legal dispute by agreements between the involved persons before the case is brought to court

trial (TRYLE)—presentation of all facts and evidence in a dispute before a judge and/or jury in a court of law